The Best Of
JACKSON BROWNE, EAGLES, NEIL YOUNG
For Guitar

Includes SUPER-TAB Notation

Arranged by ETHAN NEUBURG

C O N T E N T S

JACKSON BROWNE

EAGLES

NEIL YOUNG

Running On Empty

Words and Music by
JACKSON BROWNE

Moderately

1. Look-ing out at the road rush-ing un-der my wheels.

Look-ing back at the years gone by like so man - y sum-mer fields.

In six-ty five I was sev-en - teen _____ and run-ning up ____ One-o-one.

I don't know where _ I'm run-ning now; _ I'm just run - ning on.

6

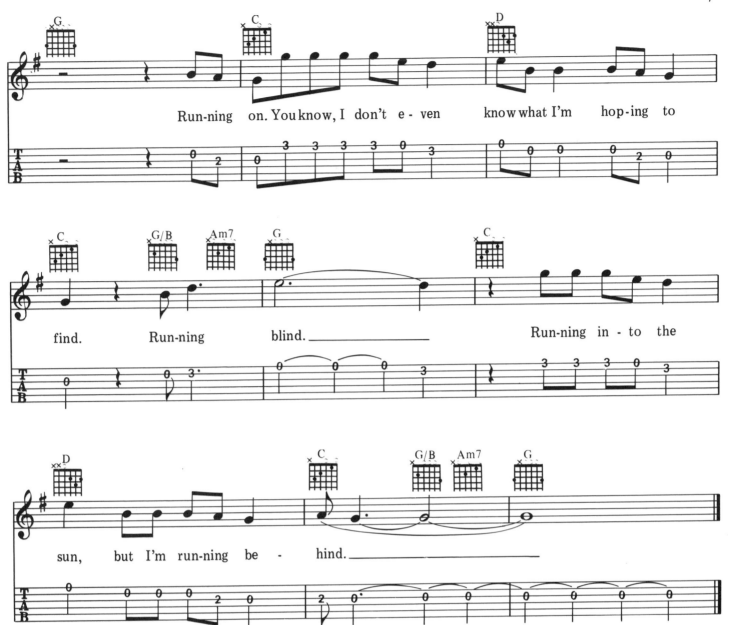

Additional Lyrics

2. Gotta do what you can just to keep your love alive,
   Trying not to confuse it with what you do to survive.
   In sixtynine I was twenty one and I called the road my own.
   I don't know when that road turned onto the road I'm on.

3. Looking out at the road rushing under my wheels.
   I don't know how to tell you all just how crazy this life feels.
   I look around for the friends that I used to turn to pull me through.
   Looking into their eyes, I see them running, too.

Hotel California

Words and Music by
DON FELDER, DON HENLEY
and GLENN FREY

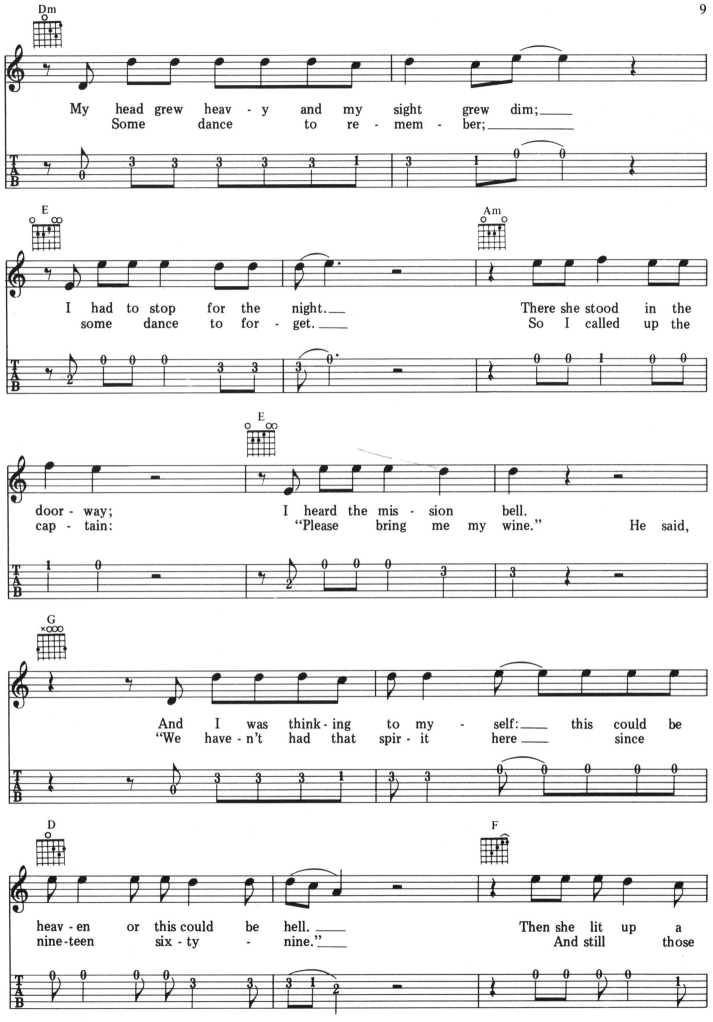

Desperado

Words and Music by
DON HENLEY and GLENN FREY

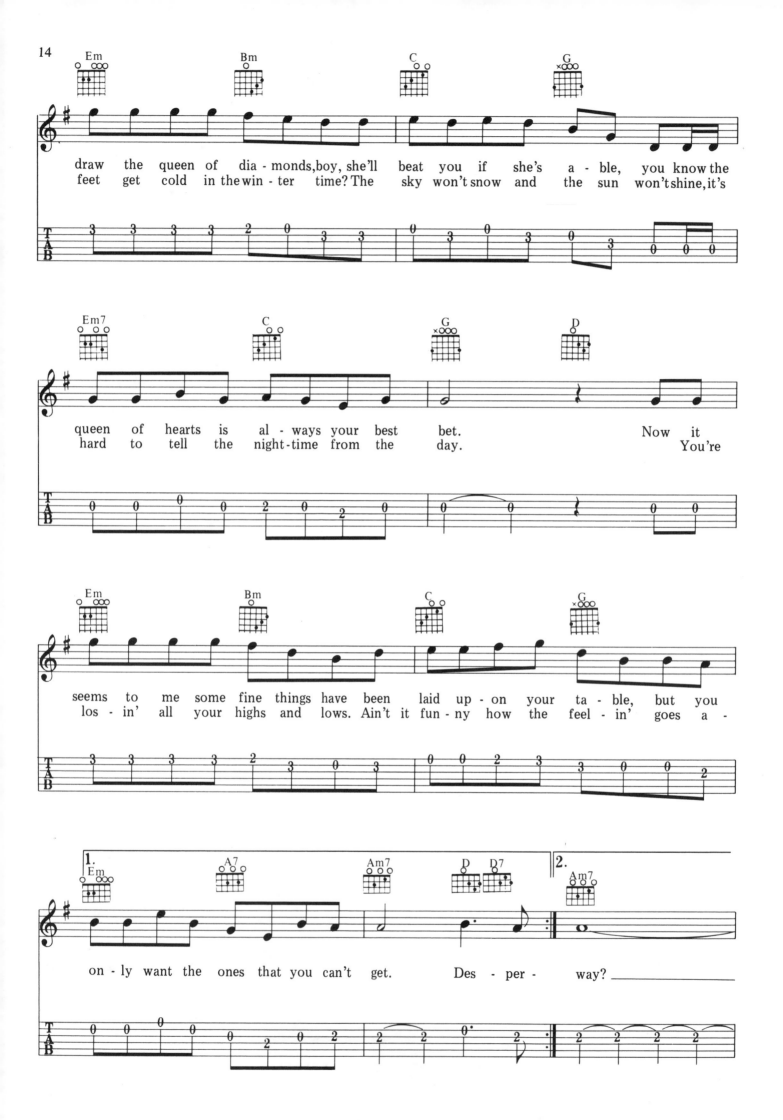

draw the queen of dia-monds,boy, she'll beat you if she's a-ble, you know the
feet get cold in the win-ter time? The sky won't snow and the sun won't shine,it's

queen of hearts is al-ways your best bet. Now it
hard to tell the night-time from the day. You're

seems to me some fine things have been laid up-on your ta-ble, but you
los-in' all your highs and lows. Ain't it fun-ny how the feel-in' goes a-

on-ly want the ones that you can't get. Des - per - way? _____

Fountain Of Sorrow

Words and Music by
JACKSON BROWNE

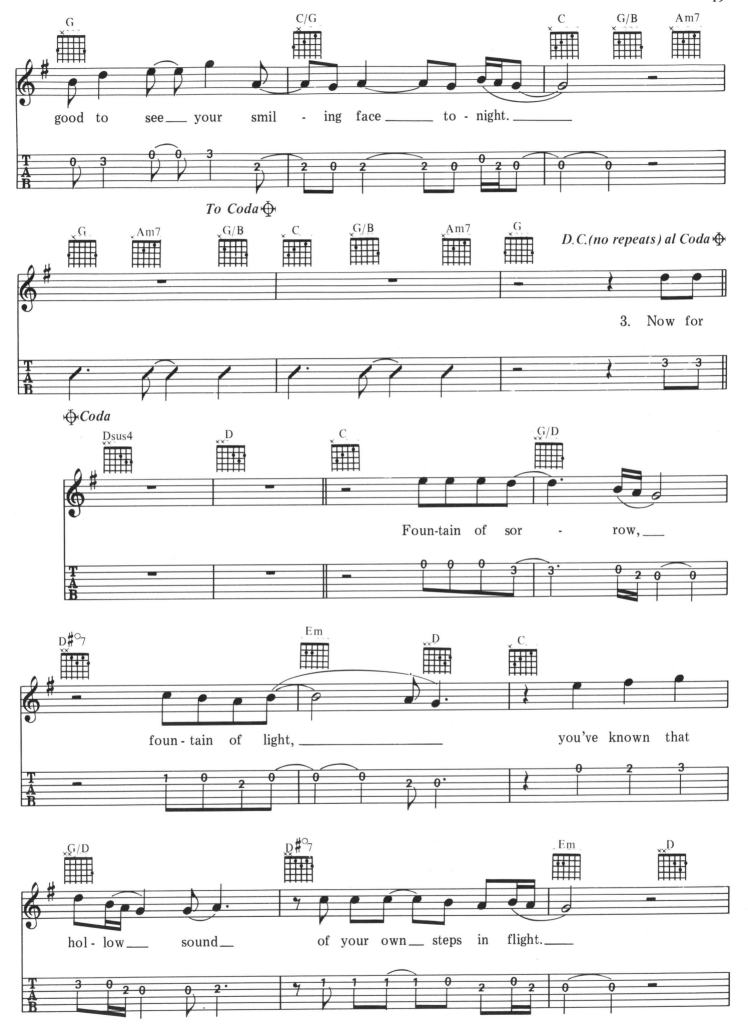

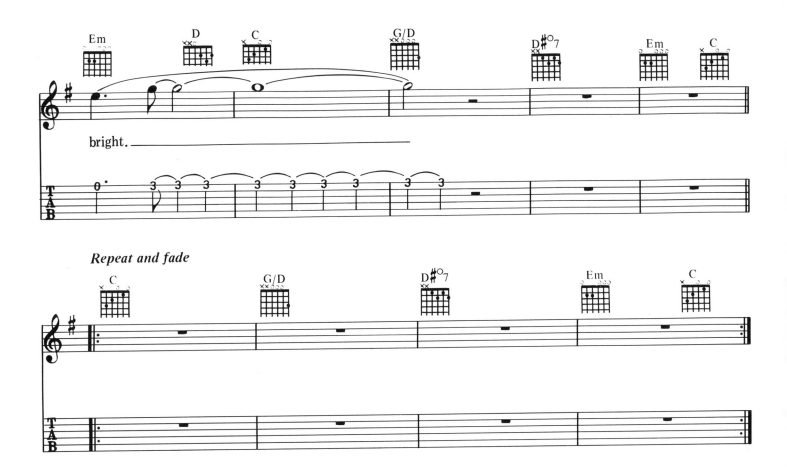

Repeat and fade

Additional Lyrics

2. Now the things that I remember seem so distant and so small,
   Though it hasn't really been that long a time.
   What I was seeing wasn't what was happening at all,
   Although for a while our path did seem to climb.
   But when you see through love's illusion, there lies the danger,
   And your perfect lover just looks like a perfect fool.
   So you go running off in search of a perfect stranger
   While the loneliness seems to spring from your life like a fountain from a pool.

Chorus

3. Now for you and me it may not be that hard to reach our dreams,
   But that magic feeling never seems to last.
   And while the future's there for anyone to change
   Still you know it seems it would be easier sometimes to change the past.
   I'm just one or two years and a couple of changes behind you,
   In my lessons at love's pain and heartache school where,
   If you feel too free and you need something to remind you,
   There's this loneliness springing up from your life like a fountain from a pool.

THE PRETENDER

Words and Music by
JACKSON BROWNE

Moderately

1. I'm gon-na rent my-self____ a house in the shade of the

free - way.____ Gon-na pack my lunch____ in the morn-ing and go to

work _____ each day. _____ And when the eve-ning rolls ____ a -

round,____ I'll go on home and lay my bod-y down. And when the

Additional Lyrics

2. I want to know what became of the changes we waited for love to bring.
   Were they only the fitful dreams of some greater awakening?
   I've been aware of the time going by.
   They say in the end, it's the wink of an eye.
   And when the morning light comes streaming in,
   You'll get up and do it again.
   Amen.

Bridge 2. I'm gonna be a happy idiot and struggle for the legal tender,
   Where the ads take aim and lay their claim to the heart and the soul of the spender,
   And believe in whatever may lie in those things that money can buy.
   Thought true love could have been a contender.
   Are you there?   Say a prayer for the pretender
   Who started out so young and strong only to surrender.

3. I'm gonna find myself a girl who can show me what laughter means.
   And we'll fill in the missing colors in each other's paint by number dreams.
   And then we'll put our dark glasses on, and we'll make love until our strength is gone.
   And when the morning light comes streaming in,
   We'll get up and do it again.
   Get it up again.

ROCK ME ON THE WATER

Words and Music by
JACKSON BROWNE

Additional Lyrics

2. The road is filled with homeless souls, every woman, child and man
   Who have no idea where they will go, but they'll help you if they can..
   But everyone must have some thought that's gonna pull them through somehow.
   Oh, the fires are raging hotter and hotter, but the sisters of the sun are gonna rock me on the water now.

3. Oh, people, look among you, it's there your hope must lie.
   There's a seabird above you gliding in one place like Jesus in the sky.
   We all must do the best we can and then hang on to that Gospel plow.
   When my life is over I'm gonna stand before the Father, but the sisters of the sun are gonna rock me
   on the water now.

Boulevard

Words and Music by
JACKSON BROWNE

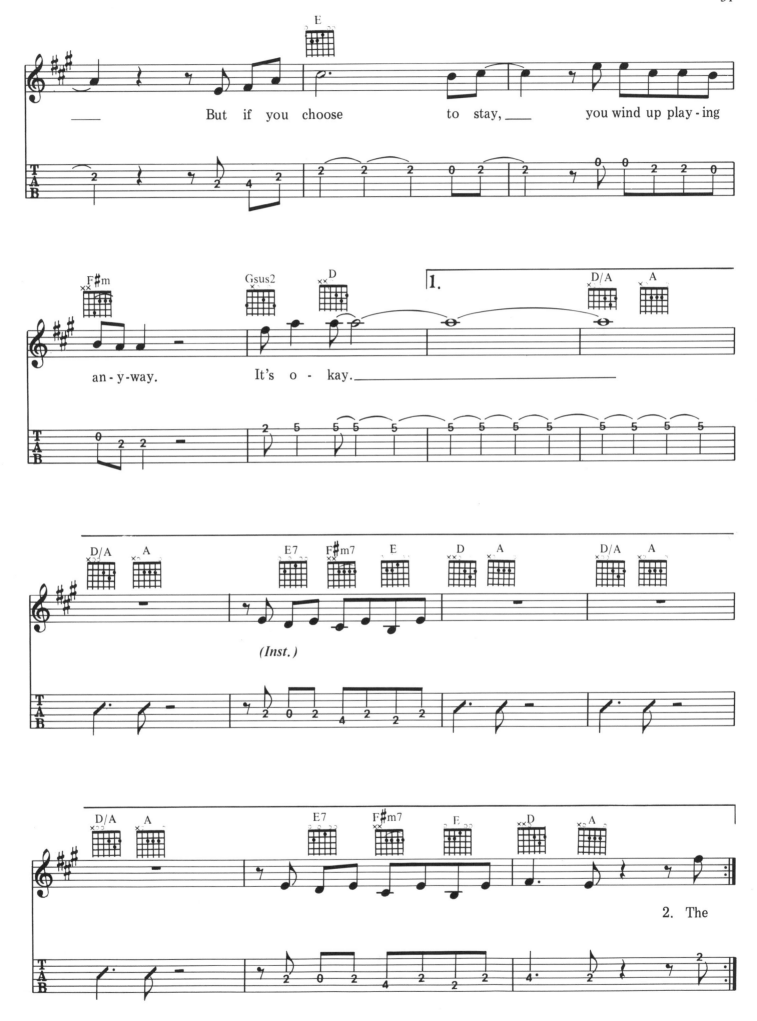

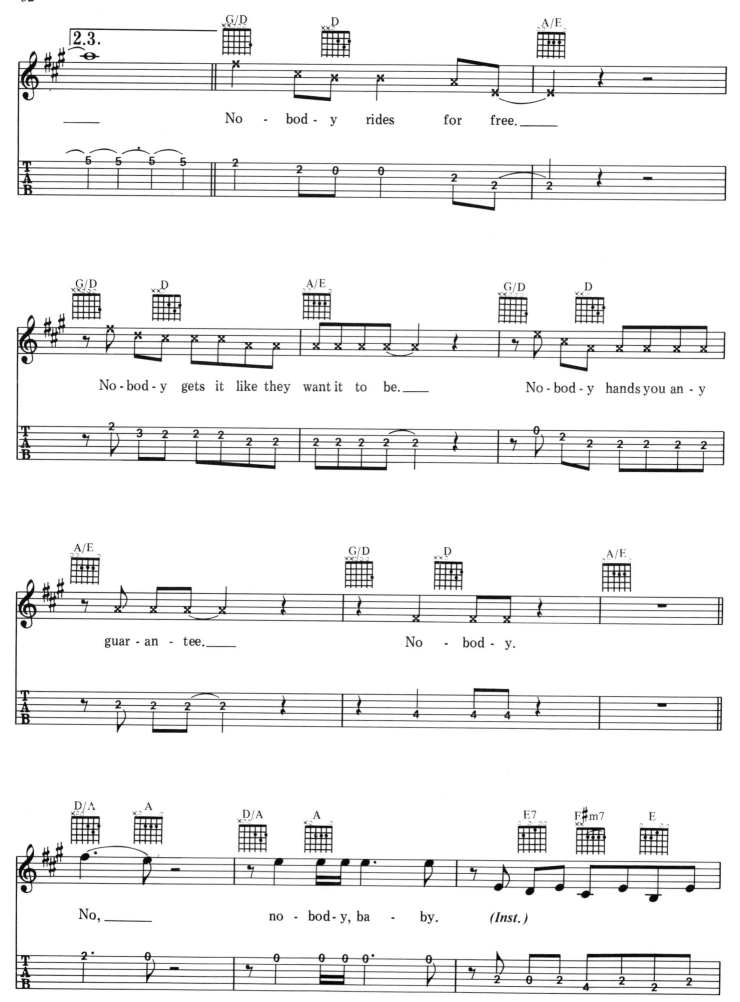

Repeat and fade

Additional Lyrics

2. The kid's in shock up and down the block.
   The folks are home playing Beat The Clock.
   Down at The Golden Cup they set the young ones up
   Under the neon light, selling day for night.
   It's alright.

3. The hearts are hard and the times are tough.
   Down on the Boulevard the night's enough.
   And time passes slow between the storefront shadows and the light's glow.
   Everybody walks right by like they're safe or something.
   They don't know.

   Nobody knows you.
   Nobody owes you nothing.
   Nobody shows you what they're thinking.
   Nobody.

   Hey, hey, baby, got to watch the street and keep your feet and be on guard.
   Make it pay, baby.
   It's only time on the Boulevard.

The Best Of My Love

Words and Music by
DON HENLEY, GLENN FREY
and JOHN DAVID SOUTHER

Ev - er - y night ___ I'm ly - in' in bed, ___
Beau - ti - ful fac - es and loud emp - ty plac - es,

hold - in' you close ___ in my dreams, ___ think - in' a - bout ___ all the
look at the way ___ that we live; ___ wast - in' our time ___ on

things that we said and com - in' a - part ___ at the seams.
cheap talk and wine left us so lit - tle to give.

We try to talk it o - ver but the words come out too ___
That same old crowd was like a cold dark cloud that we could never rise a -

HEART OF GOLD

Words and Music by
NEIL YOUNG

39

Additional Lyrics

2. I've been to Hollywood, I've been to Redwood,
I'd cross the ocean for a heart of gold.
I've been in my mind, it's such a fine line
That keeps me searchin' for a heart of gold,
And I'm gettin' old.
Keeps me searchin' for a heart of gold,
And I'm gettin' old.

Sugar Mountain

Words and Music by
NEIL YOUNG

Additional Lyrics

(Chorus)
2. There's a girl just down the aisle,
   Oh, to turn and see her smile.
   You can hear the words she wrote
   As you read the hidden note.

(Chorus)
3. Now you're underneath the stairs
   And you're givin' back some glares
   To the people who you met,
   And it's your first cigarette.

(Chorus)
4. Now you say you're leavin' home
   'Cause you want to be alone,
   Ain't it funny how you feel
   When you're findin' out it's real.
   (Chorus)

Already Gone

Words and Music by
JACK TEMPCHIN and ROBB STRANDLUND

Moderate Rock beat

1. Well, I heard some peo - ple talk - in' just __ the oth - er day, __

and they said you were gon - na put me on __ a

shelf. __ But let me tell you I got some news __ for

you __ and you'll soon find out __ it's true, and then you'll

Additional lyrics

2. The letter that you wrote me made me stop and wonder why,
   But I guess you felt like you had to set things right.
   Just remember this, my girl, when you look up in the sky
   You can see the stars and still not see the light.
   (Chorus)

3. Well, I know it was'nt you who held me down;
   Heaven knows it wasn't you who set me free.
   So oftentimes it happens that we live our lives in chains
   And we never even know we have the key.
   (Chorus)

You Love The Thunder

Words and Music by
JACKSON BROWNE

When you look _____ o - ver your shoul - der _____

and you see the life _____ that you have left be - hind;

when you think it o - ver, _____ do you ev - er won - der

what it is that holds your life so close to mine? _____

Additional Lyrics

Draw the shade and light the fire
For the night that holds you and calls your name.
And just like your lover knows your desire
And the crazy longing that time will never tame,
You love the thunder and you love the rain.
You know your hunger like you know your name.
I got your number if it's still the same.
And you can dream but you can never go back the way you came.

LOVE IS A ROSE

Words and Music by
NEIL YOUNG

49

50

Additional Lyrics

2. I wonna go to an old hoe down
Long ago in a western town.
Pick me up 'cause my feet are draggin';
Give me a lift and I'll hay your wagon.

Lyin' Eyes

Words and Music by
DON HENLEY and GLENN FREY

Bright Country style

1. Cit - y girls __ just seem to find __ out ear - ly

how to o - pen doors with just a smile.

A rich old man, __ and she won't have to wor - ry;

she'll dress up all in lace and go in style.

Additional lyrics

2. Late at night a big old house gets lonely;
   I guess every form of refuge has its price.
   And it breaks her heart to think her love is only
   Given to a man with hands as cold as ice.

3. So she tells him she must go out for the evening
   To comfort an old friend who's feelin' down.
   But he knows where she's goin' as she's leavin';
   She is headed for the cheatin' side of town.
       (Chorus)

4. She gets up and pours herself a strong one
   And stares out at the stars up in the sky.
   Another night, it's gonna be a long one;
   She draws the shade and hangs her head to cry.

5. My, oh my, you sure know how to arrange things;
   You set it up so well, so carefully.
   Ain't if funny how your new life didn't change things;
   You're still the same old girl you used to be.
       (Chorus)

After The Gold Rush

Words and Music by
NEIL YOUNG

Additional Lyrics

2. I was lyin' in a burned-out basement with the full moon in my eyes.
I was hopin' for replacement when the sun burst through the sky.
There was a band playin' in my head and I felt like getting high.
I was thinkin' about what a friend had said, I was hopin' it was a lie.
Thinkin' about what a friend had said, I was hopin' it was a lie.

3. Well, I dreamed I saw the silver spaceships flyin' in the yellow haze of the sun.
There were children cryin' and colors flyin' all around the chosen ones.
All in a dream, all in a dream, the loading had begun.
Flying Mother Nature's silver seed to a new home in the sun.
Flying Mother Nature's silver seed to a new home.

Heartache Tonight

Words and Music by
DON HENLEY, GLENN FREY, BOB SEGER
and J.D. SOUTHER

60

Cinnamon Girl

Words and Music by
NEIL YOUNG

Ma send me mon - ey now, I'm gon - na make it some -

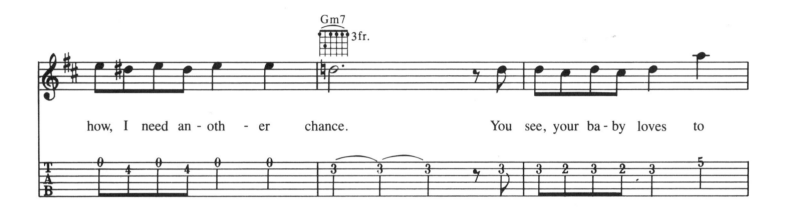

how, I need an - oth - er chance. You see, your ba - by loves to

dance, yeah, yeah, yeah.

Additional Lyrics

2. Ten silver saxes, a bass with a bow,
   The drummer relaxes and waits between shows
   For his cinnamon girl.
   A dreamer of pictures *(etc.)*

Here Come Those Tears Again

Words and Music by
JACKSON BROWNE and NANCY FARNSWORTH

The Load-Out

Words and Music by
JACKSON BROWNE and BRYAN GAROFALO

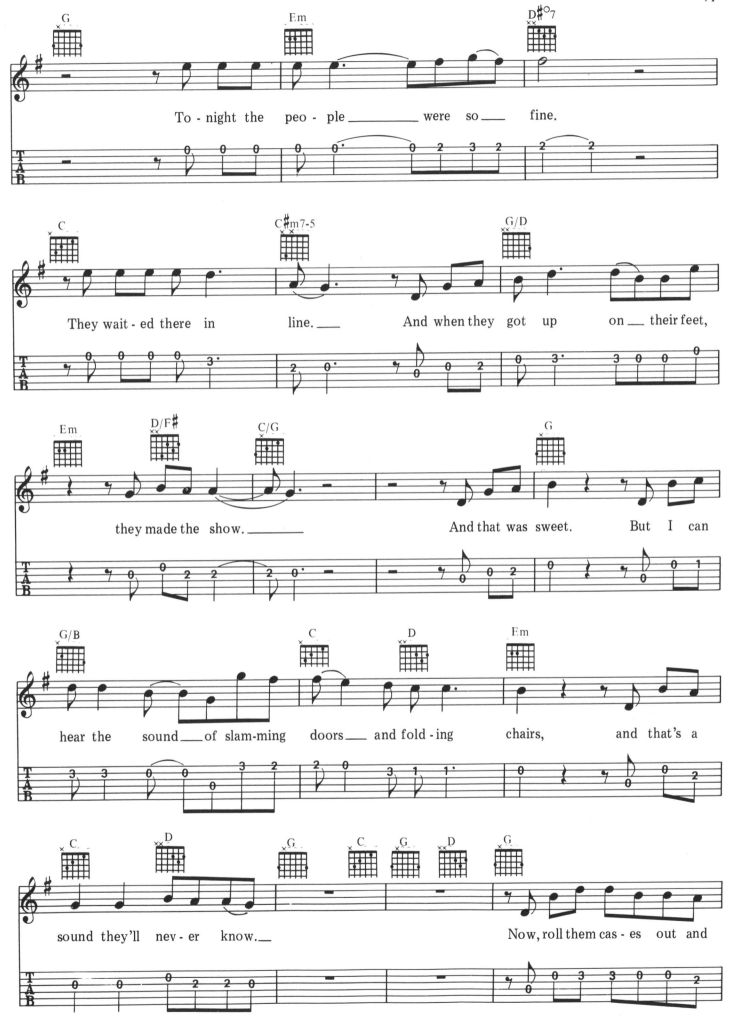

Peaceful Easy Feeling

Words and Music by
JACK TEMPCHIN

Additional lyrics

2. And I found out a long time ago
    What a woman can do to your soul;
    Ah, but she can't take you anyway,
    You don't already know how to go.
    And I got a peaceful, easy feelin', *(etc.)*

3. I get the feelin' I may know you
    As a lover and a friend;
    But this voice keeps whisperin' in my other ear,
    Tells me I may never see you again.
    'Cause I got a peaceful, easy feelin', *(etc.)*

Ohio

Words and Music by
NEIL YOUNG

Moderate March Tempo

Tin sol-diers and Nix-on com-ing; we're fi-nal-ly on our own. This sum-mer I hear the drum-ming: Four dead in O-hi-o. Got-ta get down to it, sol-diers are gun-ning us down;

Harvest

Words and Music by
NEIL YOUNG

tell you that it was on - ly a change of plan? Dream

up, dream up, let me fill your cup with the prom-ise of a man.

2. Did I

3. Will I

Additional Lyrics

2. Did I see you walking with the boys, though it was not hand in hand?
   And was some black face in a lonely place when you could understand?
   Did she wake you up *(etc.)*

3. Will I see you give more than I can take; will I only harvest some?
   As the days fly past will we lose our grasp or fuse it in the sun?
   Did she wake you up *(etc.)*

Take It To The Limit

Words and Music by
RANDY MEISNER, DON HENLEY
and GLENN FREY

OLD MAN

Words and Music by
NEIL YOUNG

Slowly, in 2

Old man, look at my life, I'm a lot like you were.

Old man, look at my life I'm a lot like you were.

1. Old man, *(see addtional lyrics)*

look at my life, twen-ty-four and there's so much more. Live a-lone in a

Additional Lyrics

2. Lullabies look in your eyes,
   Run around the same old town,
   Doesn't mean that much to me
   To mean that much to you.
   I've been first and last,
   Look at how the time goes past.
   But I'm all alone at last, rollin' home to you.

Witchy Woman

Words and Music by
BERNIE LEADON and DON HENLEY

91

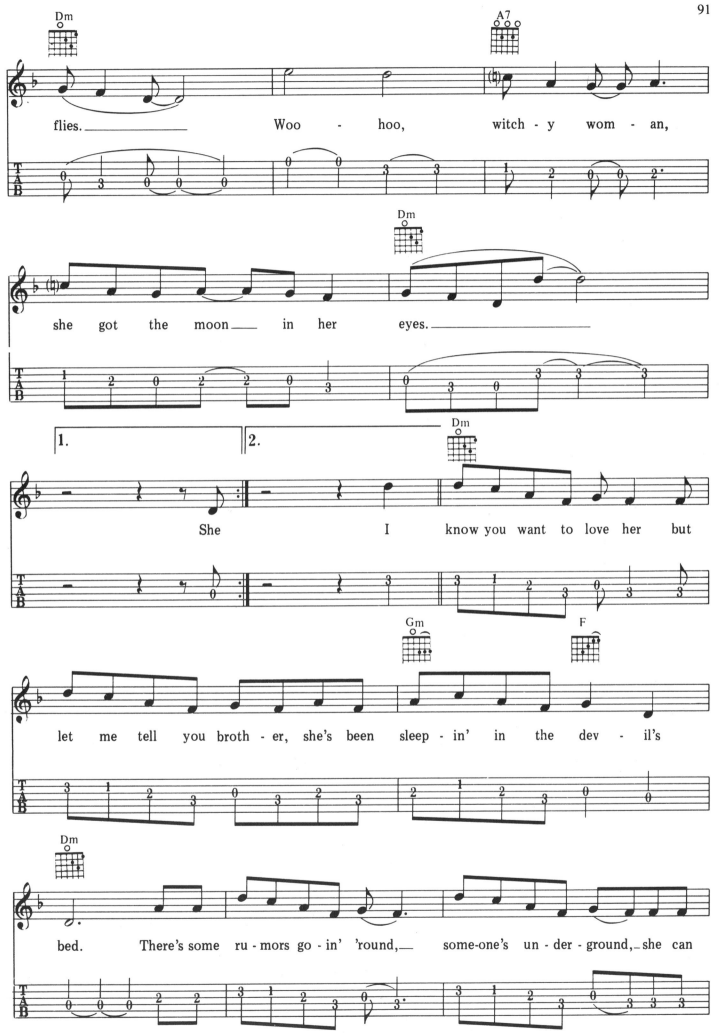

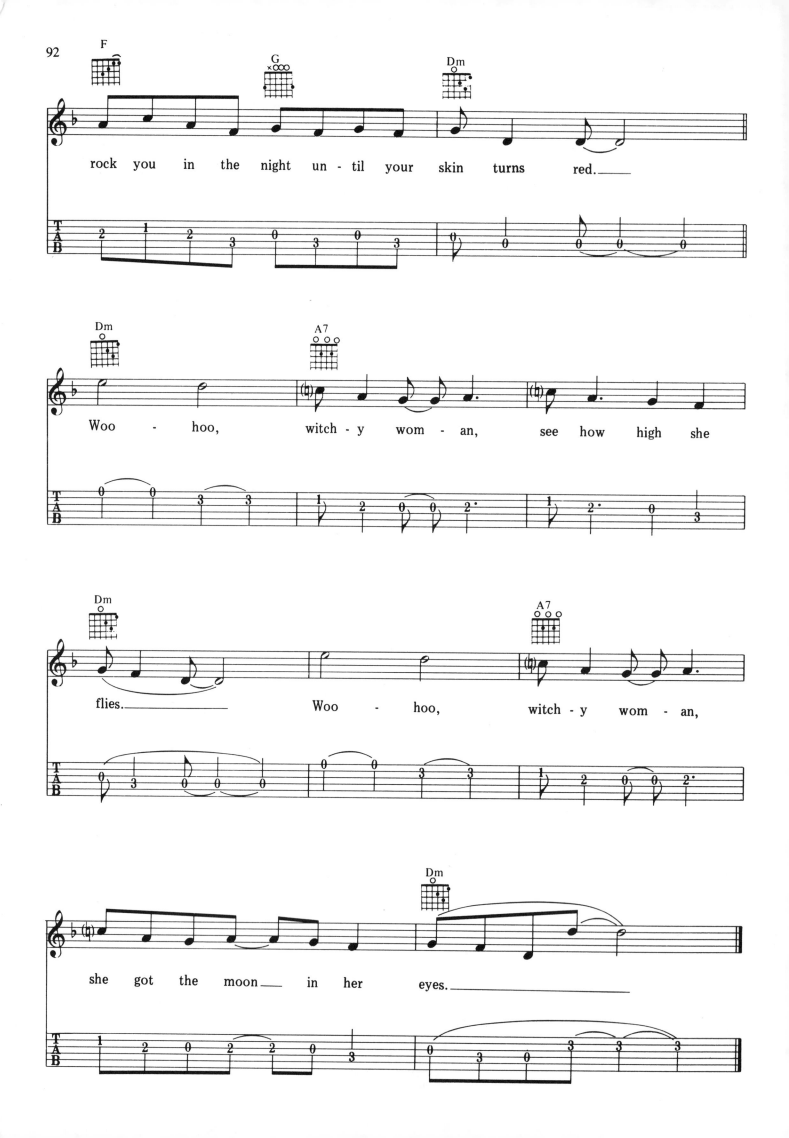

Cowgirl In The Sand

Words and Music by
NEIL YOUNG

Slowly, In 2

1. Hel - lo, cow - girl in the sand.

Is this place at your com - mand? _____

Can I stay here for a while? _____

Can I see your sweet, sweet

smile? Old e - nough, _____ now, to

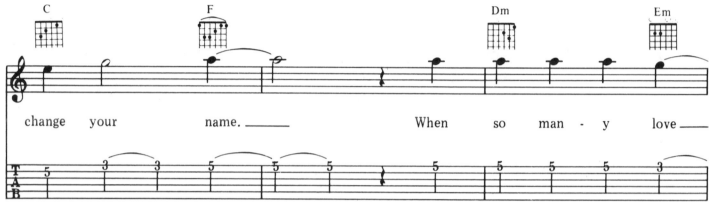

change your name. _____ When so man - y love _____

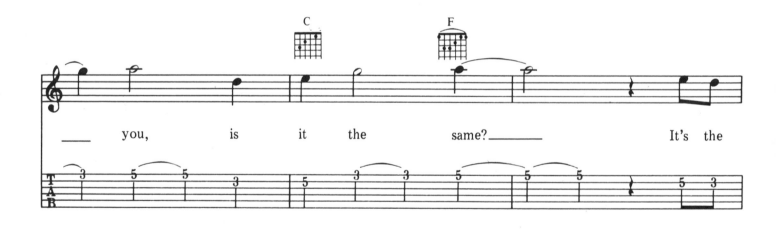

_____ you, is it the same? _____ It's the

wo - man in you that makes you want to play this game. _____

(Instrumental)

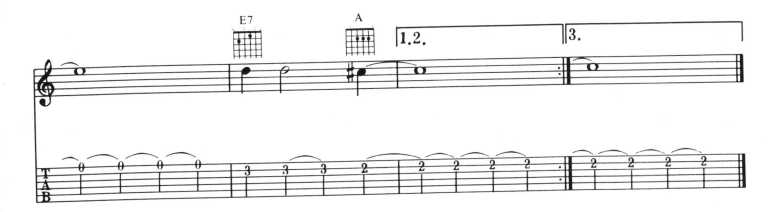

Additional Lyrics

2. Hello, ruby in the dust.
   Has your band begun to rust?
   After all the sin we've had,
   I was hoping that we'd turn bad.
   Old enough *(etc.)*

3. Hello, woman of my dreams.
   Is this not the way it seems?
   Purple words on a gray background,
   To be a woman and to be turned down.
   Old enough *(etc.)*